Under cover
of day

Under cover of day

Poems by
Tim Lenton

PAUL DICKSON BOOKS

Under cover of day

Poems by **Tim Lenton**, published by Paul Dickson Books, May 2022.

Paul Dickson Books, 156 Southwell Road, Norwich NR1 3RP,
t. 01603 666011,
e. paul@pauldicksonbooks.co.uk,
www.pauldicksonbooks.co.uk

ISBN 978-1-7397154-1-0

A CIP catalogue record for this booklet is available from the British Library.
Printed in Norwich by GoWise Print

Foreword

These poems were written largely between 2010 and 2020. They reflect various places and styles. Although I enjoy writing to a strict structure, as in haiku and tanka (published largely elsewhere) most of my poems are based mainly on rhythm (I am a great admirer of Gerard Manley Hopkins) and aim to be accessible and a bit mysterious at the same time.

Life is in many ways a mystery, and to ignore this will make writing in verse forms too facile and unrewarding. But the poet must have a philosophy of life – a belief, if you like – that attempts to make some sense of the mystery. This often happens through juxtaposition of unlikely events or observations.

Language is fascinating, and translation even more so. I don't really believe poetry can be translated effectively, because it is impossible to transfer all the subtleties of idioms and multi-meanings into another language. That is why the Bible in English is capable of so much misinterpretation, having been written originally in Hebrew or Aramaic – two languages whose words contain so much subtlety and multiplicity of meanings.

Poems – even simple poems – must have a certain depth to make them worthwhile. But of course different readers will enjoy swimming at different depths. My aim as a poet is to make my words deep enough, but not too deep –rather as Einstein urged us to make everything as simple as possible, but not simpler.

I don't like too much punctuation cluttering up a poem, which is why I rarely use full stops. I prefer to use the verse structure to indicate where a sentence ends, and I find that a colon often does the job – but only in the context of poetry!

Tim Lenton
February 2022

For Dot, David, Oliver and Amy

Contents

Introduction

These are introductory notes to a selection of the poems.

Italian time was written during a holiday in Tuscany in 2010. *Blink* was written after a visit to The Rosary, my favourite cemetery, while I was recovering from a gall bladder infection during the pandemic of 2020. It refers to a particularly memorable episode of Doctor Who, with the same title. *Burnham Norton* is on the north coast of Norfolk. *When my father was alive* is set in Beanfield Avenue, Coventry, where we lived for a while in the early 1950s. *Passing place* was inspired by a beautiful road between Crathie and the Bridge of Gairn in Aberdeenshire.

From a distance was inspired by the long, lovely walk to Blakeney Point from Cley in North Norfolk. *Failure to connect*, by contrast, reflects my first contact with Iona, off the west coast of Scotland. *Films about bears* was prompted by a visit to Walsingham in Norfolk, which boasts a shrine and snowdrops, but no bears. *North wall* is that of the Eiger in Switzerland.

Limit of navigation was written after a walk in north-east Norfolk close to Honing and the North Walsham and Dilham Canal. *Deceiving the eye* had its birth in a holiday in Catalonia, where we visited a museum housing Dali's work in Figueras. *Prime summits* reflects my not always simultaneous interest in mountains and numbers, and *Croagh Patrick*, of course, came from a walk up this iconic Irish mountain associated with St Patrick.

Lockdown is a very recent poem relating of course to the 2020 pandemic and its continual uncertainty. *Drawn to the edge* is much earlier, prompted by a visit to Lyme Park and a walk to the Macclesfield Canal, Lancashire, in 2011. *Birds in the distance* was inspired by a flying visit to an area near Henley-on-Thames. *Failing fire* won a competition organised by Norwich Writers' Circle in 2011.

Edge of eternity followed another hospital visit, and *Dancing with Teresa di Avila* was sparked by a talk on mystics given online by Mirabai Starr. *After hearing Adam Cohen* followed a superb if informal concert at the University of East Anglia, and *Just like Lazarus* was sparked by walking in Norwich Cathedral, where many footsteps are slowly deleting the names on floor-laid tombstones. Two of my close friends are remembered in *Like a hero* and *Passing through*. Dave Gemmell was a well-known writer of science fantasy who I worked with (before he became famous) on the Acton Gazette in London, and David Coomes was another work colleague, this time at The Christian newspaper, also in London. He later became well known in BBC radio, where he produced The Moral Maze.

Regardless was inspired by a concert in Orford, Suffolk: one of the small boats in the bay was called Regardless. *Your silence* is about my wife, who should have inspired more poetry. Unfortunately she is poetry, and you can't easily write good poetry about poetry. *After the third field* harks back to my childhood and a strange dream I had where I wanted to open my eyes, but knew I couldn't because it was a dream.

Young birds was highly commended in a Suffolk competition judged by Martin Figura, who said some nice things about it. *This is not it* was provoked by another stay in hospital. I have twice woken up in hospital in the middle of the night and believed I was elsewhere. Quite frightening. *Walking at my own speed* came from a coastal walk near Cley, in North Norfolk, with my son David and grandchildren Oliver and Amy. *God's angle* was inspired by my granddaughter.

Seagull was seen through my kitchen window: the king in the last line is of course the bird itself. *Song for a moment* was inspired by my two favourite songwriters and the landscape around my favourite Scottish loch. *Anne Boleyn's window* is in Hever Castle, where we stayed for a weekend, and *Boneland* was prompted by a walk near Holt, and of course by the poetic novel of the same name by Alan Garner. *The rise and fall* is North Norfolk again, but *Playing with fish* is Florida – Captiva Island, to be precise, where we were taken on holiday by friends and fell in love (with the island).

Goats in the machine is of course a play on words – the words of Arthur Koestler, who wrote Ghost in the Machine, though the original words are not original to him. *Age of steam* came from a short journey in Yorkshire on the Sir Nigel Gresley, a sister steam engine to the record-holding Mallard, and a thing of rare beauty. Thanks to Julia and Dave Evetts for introducing us to it, and to many other things.

Proof of heaven took place in a private swimming pool at Montauroux in the South of France, courtesy of our best man, Fred Riches, and his wife. For *Bluebell* we are back again in The Rosary.

Italian time

Stranded at Lamole
in Italian time,
where hours stretch and crinkle
under the Chianti sun,

you take a last sip of limoncello
and reach for the lizard
on the water's edge,
hoping to save it from drowning

Your hand touches;
the reptile recoils

You swoop to scoop it out,
but you come at it
from the wrong direction

It spills from your slippery fingers
into the pool overflow
and plunges down

Now when you come to save me from drowning
in these whispering hills,
I will know the importance
of where I stand,
the direction you come from,
and the speed of the overflow

In Italian time
under the Chianti sun
I am practising stillness,
so that when your finger touches me
I give way softly,

and recoil
is no longer a problem

Blink

Tombstones lean forward to kiss the earth
losing their balance in the unexpected sun

An accidental tree
wraps itself like a sheet across the horizon
and a man in a faded shirt sits by the path
waiting for the next day, and the day after

A young woman with straight hair saunters
down the winding track through the woods,
turns on to the road, walks, then disappears
like a dream

and I feel tiredness wash down my body,
spilling on to the dry grass

I can go no further:
I close my eyes while the stone angels creep closer,
and I am transported back in time,
but nothing changes

I hold out my hand
and feel the touch of the future,
relieved
that it is still there

Burnham Norton

I stop at Burnham Norton
halfway to nowhere
and listen to the stillness of the marsh

Down its invisible paths
white flowers open,
soak up the sun:

dunes in the distance
like border guards checking the sea,
a windmill standing sentry

I imagine a woman walking down
from Brancaster,
watching the red kites,
her clothes matching the colour
of their wings

And on the hill, ruins
of the ancient friary,
its winding stairs,
its open window
and its unmade bed,
all to the glory of God

I can say no more:
down Blacksmiths Lane
even the children are silent

British winter time

The sky draws a line under lifeless clouds
as if the day is over:
witch-green, layered time
stepping meanly backwards,
hiding the light
behind jailer voices
while meadowed horses wait to be released

and the promised hour is swallowed
by grey land – old hoofprints
heading plainly for the flood,
reeds bent endlessly in prayer

across a path too often travelled
into the northern mist
towards the december sea

When my father was alive

Sixty years on, the trains
still run at the bottom of my garden

I return, expecting to see
uprooted rails, something for walkers,
a crazed cycle path,

but I hear the train, and I see
the track, though the meadows it ran through
have been shaved and smartened
into a blazered sports field, and a fence
blocks my old path to the dark woods

I search for signs of my childhood,
marks I might have made

Someone has thrown away the broken tooth
and the bicycle,

and the moon my father chased up the street
got away – as did the boy
who pulled his toy from underneath a moving car
while I stood transfixed

But the numbers remain:
the pavements, the houses, the steps towards school

The scene of my first major crime
(grand theft marble)
has been wiped clean
like my sins

No more lovely young girls,
no more shotguns,
no more holes in the ground

Everything is neat now,
except the forces' club and its
car park in no-man's-land,
leaking on to the street, as it always did

Swinging on some railings by the iron road,
I dropped a magic red magnet
and could never find it

Perhaps that is what draws me back
to this unremarkable street,
this shadowed and temperamental sky

under which strange things happened
to someone I almost knew

Passing place

In the wild land
between Ben Avon and Gairnshiel
between black snow and white wind
there is a passing place

where spirit brushes flesh
clouds shift shapes
and brown is the colour
of my true love's eyes

In the heather, footprints can just be seen
reaching upwards, almost hidden:
the road like a juggler
throws, then catches

nine times out of ten,
and I keep passing

This is the place:
enchantment is a wound
that reopens

I pass again

From a distance

Seen from the dunes - the Long Hills -
seen, that is to say, from a distance,
the wet sand folds like silk towards the sea

Close to me now, your body,
still like silk after all these years,
ripples under my fingers

The tide is low: the figures at the water's edge
silhouetted in the glow
beneath a darkening sky
seem fragile, at the mercy of foreign forces
yet to be unleashed

The blue building where we danced
Is lost in the maze of paths behind us:
where sand meets shingle
small birds swoop
too fast to follow

So hard to find the right person,
the sweet spot
the undeserved ecstasy

Miles behind us, our footprints
sink into the shore
and the murmur on the beach
fades into another realm

We head into a cloud of unknowing –
not willingly, not sure of the paths
that kiss the marshes

Not sure where it all ends,
if it does end –
if there is a conclusion –
if there is firm ground

But my skin and your fingers
are like a well-oiled machine
with their own language and rituals
here and now –
seen, that is to say, from a distance

Failure to connect

Skin stretched tight,
the island bares its knuckles,
holds us in the long light evening
after the ferry vanishes
as we try to connect
but fail

The corncrakes cry
but do not reveal themselves:
off the machair
sea monsters break cover
but say nothing

Narrow paths lead to the shining sound,
but there is no way out

The illusion of Fionnphort persists,
and a coloured dove
flies slowly through fire and bracken
at the abbey

It is Pentecost: a time
of healing, but it is
too late – miracles have turned
to stone

There is a chameleon in the undergrowth:
we can see its footprints

In the north-east white sand falls
into shaded blue
beyond a wild flower meadow

A storm over Mull
blows through

Films about bears

Beyond the priory
and the courtroom where the money is counted,
spring stretches its wings,
waking just for a day
like an artist faking
his own pictures, then hiding them
in the newly boarded attic
until the time is right

The picture you see
is not me: a shelf portrait
achingly safe among the snowdrops
when I should be making
films about bears
in the high country

The charge in winter batteries
does not hold
as it did earlier

They once shot trespassers here
and entertained ruinous kings:
much good it did them

We are all traitors now
keeping our heads
saving our energy

in case a bear floats by

North wall

Going higher
we leave behind
the comfortable clutter
seductive streets
the worldwide web
ouroboros

We disentangle ourselves
from all that –
the suffering of life
the unpassable pain,
the dry, illuminative way

We step on hard rock now,
edge through
where there is no other way,
expose ourselves,
nerves shining, stretched
on the north wall

And beneath the unnatural
windows
a glacier sweeps down:
we ache to be part of it,
defiant, pure, irresistible -
out in that healing cold,
the patterned valley so far away

All will be well:
there is mercy in this solitary ice

We stand like a sphinx
knowing everything
and nothing

Our fingernails crack
failing to grasp
the implications:
sun reflects off snow
while two angels
hide in plain sight

Compline

Standing on the rooftop
head against the pillar
I watch distant hills
where stars dance
and strange sounds echo

There is ice in the air
and in the forecasts:
without movement, the earth will die
and so will I

The night is long:
even the prophets have gone to bed
and the dust of death
surrounds me

The darkness is hard to take
night after night, and
all nights become one
out here in the high country

Yes, I am a watchman
and a prophet too
if truth be told:
I stand at the crossroads

Once again I see movement
in the hills
black against black
shadow against shadow

I think I see you in the distance, but
your sudden shape beside me
becomes wood and walls,
and it is night again

Pictures in my mind drown out
the voice of the trumpet:
I watch for dawn
when there will be no pictures

no hate and
no lies,
no going out
and no coming in

No secrets, because
there will be too much light

I ache for the morning
when warmth returns and
everything changes,
even my life, my
unimaginable dreams

Limit of navigation

Pulled by the pain of wind and tide
and racked by rain
your body moves from side to side

You toss and touch the shallows
gather in the sheets
tumble face down, indiscreet

Naked to sand and stone, so close
to land: pillow fair head
stranded on some quite unexpected bed

Hours tumble past,
the fast hours of the fairy moon
that drew you in

Your damp skin sinks in sightless sleep
no rise and fall outside the deep

Deceiving the eye
(Dali's jewellery)

If an angel were crucified
in the eye of time,
lines and light
would vanish into the darkness

and you would see
something else
something more believable

like an elephant from space,
a butterfly
or a night spider
crouched over an incandescent egg

Unlike the angel,
you have quick hands and free will:
you can see what you like

a royal heart pulsing, perhaps:
an explosion
dangerously close
to the tree of life

jewels in the dusk,
new wine and the gala of
immortal life

Outside, the Catalonian sun
reassures the seeker:
there is more than one way of looking
at what is not there

Prime summits

A series of summits spreads across the sky
spaced like prime numbers
making music
through their almost random placement

There is no proof of this
only conjecture
but its beauty is insistent
in the lowering light of the sun

And somewhere in there
is an impossible number
clinging by its fingertips
to unforgiving rock

There is a lady too
silent and mysterious
her undiscovered figure
keeping the universe in motion

Croagh Patrick

After forty days
the snakes left the mountain
and the land was free of evil
for a while

Now barefoot on the sharp stones
of Croagh Patrick
pilgrims try to touch the past

fingering the statue
reaching for the shadow of the bell,

then look out at the present:
islands like pages of poetry
dropped In Clew Bay

They see the whole world
floating there
dressed in blue and dying

written like magic, irresistible
waiting for a saint
to sail north

Lockdown

I am away
from the hurl and burly of life:
I lurk in my house,
watching the enemy go by

The street is empty:
my enemy is invisible –
he may kill me
or he may not

I cannot hold your hand
or comfort you
in case the enemy leaps
from your back to mine

He may leap
or he may not

He is not in my house
as far as I know

He may be
or he may not:
he may have been
and gone

There is no way
of knowing

The sun is shining
but I cannot leave my house:
I am probably too old –
I may be
or I may not

There is no hurl and burly of life
anywhere:
everyone is in their houses

They cannot go out:
they have forgotten the password

They may retrieve it
or they may not

God has the key:
He may throw it to us –
we may catch it,
or we may not

Drawn to the edge

The sun plays hide-and-seek among hilltop trees
firing its paintball light
onto the valley water,
inventing strange angles and impossible colours

while shadow ice coats cracking valley walls
like deep-sea teeth
anchored in cold blood

and geese skate like ghosts down the canal,
breaking the fragile surface,
reflecting, plunging in,
pretending to carry it off, not really surprised,
as if they meant it

As twilight sidles in, I am drawn to the edge
as if I mean it,
but wanting to fly, not skate or swim – fly in the evening hilltop air,
arms wide, chasing the nearest star,
looking for that lost ladder up to heaven

I do not carry it off:
instead I watch baby eagles
plunging past light and ice
outside the nest,
falling, but never quite
hitting the ground,

discovering wings.

At the chemist's

They are for her stomach, she says,
but she cannot remember their name:
the box was purple, perhaps, and
they may or may not have begun with m

Yes, she has come down from the mountain
for her Christmas tablets,
to which she is legally entitled:
tablets of the law

But I, living under grace,
get my tablets free, at any time,
and I know their name
as well as the colour of the box

I do not boast about it
because the New Testament forbids
boasting

Nor do I boast of knowing
the shape of the paracetamol my wife requires:
she has difficulty swallowing,
but I know exactly what she will swallow

I tell her tomorrow will be
two minutes, twelve seconds shorter,
and she does not find this hard to believe
or stomach,
what with the iconoclastic ice on the pavement
and the darkness that is almost biblical

The chemist emerges from his mysterious caverns
with a bundle of embarrassing size
and hands it to me
as if I had conceived it out of wedlock

which is impossible
for many reasons

The immaculate tablets keep me alive,
but that is no excuse:
I have kept people waiting

I should have gone for resurrection:
the whole hog, no messing

Either you believe in God
or you don't

Birds in the distance

In red kite country, above the church,
he kicks at dead leaves
and climbs the ancient face of a hill
cloaked with skin-tight trees

Gold pieces scatter
from pockets of denim sky
always just out of reach

and a note on a broken fence says
'Grandad, I miss you so much'

The day is slipping away,
never to be seen again,
however much loving it contained

and the summit is still out there
in the encroaching dark

He pauses where the path divides,
sure he sees a woman with black hair
and a holier spirit,

birds in the distance
as the sun
irresistibly
sets

Failing fire

In these soft, grey, collapsing January days
where dawn and dusk meet on main street at noon
too weak, too low to draw their weapons
and life seeps away
like air from a pricked balloon,

the fire fails:
faint flames lick the edges
of lime logs, traces of orange
in the colluding coals

There was a blaze here once,
not quite a furnace –
no iron forged, no tons of nails for tall adventuring ships –
but enough to warm a visitor or two

You held out your hands sometimes and felt
some subtle change in temperature

Now I close one eye as I write:
mist spills uneasily out of my dreams,
dancing through my bones,
piercing or tickling my spirit

interrupting the invisible sun
while a cold wind across the cemetery
digs deeper

keeping the fire going
or putting it out

Edge of eternity

I stand on the edge of eternity:
a door opens, and I look back at the universe,
which sparkles and throbs with life

I know I must not touch
the angel at the door
of creation

If I do, I will have to go on
into the realm of angels,
but back there in the coruscating night
people are calling to me

I still belong
in that crazy fairground

I do not know why
or how I can help,
or what I have done so far

I reached out
but no-one responded

I like the look of the angel
at the door of creation, and
the angel smiles at me

I do not touch him:
all I want is beauty,
or is it holiness?

I do not touch the angel

I look again at eternity:
the nurse comes
to give me painkillers

Dead lucky

Walking through the obituaries
I ask myself
what kind of person I will have been:
guitarist, poet, diplomat,
lover, joker, thief…

What will they say?
I struggle to think of a headline, or
even an opening paragraph

I meet a professor of death studies
and ask him if he really exists on this level
or merely afterwards

Am I anything special?
A ghost would be something:
there are people I would love to haunt
for different reasons

Last night I saw you through your bedroom window
and walked away,
although I know
that angels exist

I did not save children from an earthquake
by allowing a wall to fall on me
I did not breathe deeply and
bring my neighbour back to life

I did not capture a hill
from the enemy

I spoke in tongues and
would have given everything for you
but it seemed extreme, and anyway
you didn't ask

I was a fool because
I failed to give what could not be kept
for what could not be lost

But God loves even fools:
I cling on to an outstretched arm
and will be rescued
from fire and flood

No-one will write about it, though –
not even the professor

A few angels
may sing

Dancing with Teresa di Avila

For ever, she said,
and could not stop saying it:
I look into the future
and she is still there

a guide through the landscape of loss
on the edge
hitting the ground flying
wisdom keeper and drama queen

If you ask her questions
she will seduce you
Jew and Carmelite
going to the well

She digs ditches
creates wheels of water
and grace falls, flowing
through the interior castle

For ever, she says

After hearing Adam Cohen

So far from Montreal,
you smoke a cigarette with your back against the low black building
where you sang your surreal songs,
and we sat at civilised tables

I want to talk to you about your matchbox
and about that woman who you thanked
for being so beautiful,
but I don't know what to say

'I knew your father'
doesn't seem to do it:
I don't know how you feel about your father –
is he competition, distraction
or inspiration?

Poetry is in your blood:
it flows from that wound in your side,
and the pages turn red so easily

In that respect we are similar,
but I never knew Marianne:
I know your father, though – better than I knew mine:
mine died young

You will move on, and I will remain
wading through the songs my father sang
looking for ways to understand
the maps he used, and the hard
landscape he travelled through

The gift of blood keeps us both alive:
your voice refreshes me, like water, and
your bus pulls out on to the road

On my way home I pass the houses
where my father and mother were born
and the church where they met and married,

so far from Montreal,
so far

Just like Lazarus

Even your name has been erased:
trodden out of existence
by dull cathedral visitors

and you beneath it all
unluckily forgotten
while blind survivors manage so easily
without you

like a jigsaw with a vital piece missing
but somehow, unbelievably, complete

Were you ever needed at all?
Exiled to the caverns of your imagination
you run your fingers through the dust

and hope
that someone, weeping,
will eventually come along

and see that you are just like Lazarus:
not that far in,
and aching to be recalled

Early snow

Halfhearted flakes float down like a string
of objectors parachuted in
behind the lines:

conscientious but in love with the sun,
they would rather not be there
and intend to slip away quietly
under cover of day

Like a hero

(for Dave Gemmell)

Leafing through my past,
I stumble on your name
and remember your stories
of dream and reality

I hear the echoes
of that great song,
finger the long edge of the legendary sword,
feel the shiver up my spine again,

the touch of the game
and the secrets:
other people's nakedness and ours:
the mix of wine,

the time I cracked
but you decided not to kill me,
seeing the berserker inside...

I was in the bath, spilling time,
when news of your death reached me:
your heart had been repaired
but failed without warning

The human condition: truth
does not have to make sense

You had been afraid at the end
but like a hero:
tempted in the wilderness,
reaching for that one blue shining
unfilmed afternoon

Passing through
(for David Coomes)

One morning early,
before what used to be breakfast,
you sigh finally, like a breeze,
step out of the moral maze
and into something quite new,
unproduced, unscripted

The pain disappears,
not gradually but all at once,
replaced by something cool and warm
and healing:
something quite new

Through unexpected channels
you give birth to yourself, look round,
breathe out:
someone is holding you
and there is no sea

The touching clumsiness of old life falls away, and
you move in different directions,
impossibly free

You reach out for heaven again
and touch it
easily

Regardless

Where the road turns and heads for the quay
music leaks out of the church,
through the ruined arches
and into the village

Noah and the dove watch it
flood and fall back,
cellos marching past the waterfall
of the flute,
one orchestra against another

The mystery of the music spans centuries,
and the castle, off to one side,
hears it too

Notes and scales drift out into the wrecks of buildings
that punctuate the Ness,
abandoned after the war,
waiting for artists to roll the stones away
and resurrect some kind of beauty

Eventually the magic fades:
small boats jog lightly in the harbour
regardless

haiku

your unmade bed, white
through the window: I watch from
your apple garden

too heavy to fly,
the dreams of an angry man
perish in the storm

After the third field

After the third field
there is a wood,
which is mysterious to a child
who thinks fields should continue

In the wood there are twisted limbs
and paths that circle
going nowhere

The two of them sit in the wood
near the rhododendron
and consider the situation:
is this a dream or not?

He tries to open his eyes,
but it is impossible:
she calls from an open window

They look back from the wood
across three fields,
and across the years:
the fields are filled with buildings

The only way to reach the wood now
is from the other side
where there is no magic

Your silence

I lie beside you in the darkness
and try to hear you breathe:
the waves beat on the winter beach
but you are silent like the sky

I strain to catch some movement
against the invisible sheets:
the shingle shifts beneath the breath of the sea
but you are still like a sail in the sunset

I want to touch you
to feel your beating waves and shifting shingle
but I do not want to disturb
the child inside the universe

I cannot sleep

Young birds

Light flashes in the hedge
as young birds
free from the fields
taste the edges of their new world

then come to feed from our fingers:
sunlight pierces their wings
and the puzzle of leaves and branches
as we watch,

remembering Columba
the holy dove
and the flames of light
that settled on him, filled his house

full of love and secrets,
consuming the dry, tender land

Liturgy

You smiled at me when we met
suddenly in the cathedral
but later you turned away
as if afraid

that it might become a habit
and we might walk for ever
down the aisles, or
in the sunny labyrinth
outside

The risk of smiling
at someone you might not know
became too great,
the liturgy too
frighteningly real

This is not it

There is blood on my pillow:
it is raining outside

Moving closer to hell,
away from the window,
bared to the random beeps and whistles
of determined devils
that burrow into the unbalanced mind,
disrupting the harmony of the cosmos,
rejecting glory,

I wake again to this emptiness –
this brash and pointless conversation,
self-obsessed,
echoing in grey and lifeless rooms

Is this what remains
when you remove the pain?
A quiet man struggling to his feet,
curtains drawn across reality,
prayers looking for the light?

Or is it something outside –
something unreachable?

Bizarre constructions fall apart,
rebuild themselves,
and the old, old man sinks further into his pillow,
finger pointing feebly at water
like some kind of creator
whose power has drained away

We are all waiting to leave,
drifting into what may or may not be the future,
hoping that God will burst in and say:

This is not it:
you should not be here

Follow me

Walking at my own speed

Walking at my own speed
I set out across the marshes
on the fringe of time

My son and grandson tread the raised path
ahead of me
past broken fences bleached by the sun
tidal pools pricked by a western wind
and an old house perched uneasily
on the shifting shingle

They start off close to me,
my flesh and blood, then – walking at their own speed –
advance into the distance
until I can scarcely distinguish
who they are,
two shadows against the sun

We walked together once:
I showed them mountain roads
and valleys by the sea,
but now, assured, they leave me easily behind,
which is as it should be:
eventually I shall slow down even more and stop,
perhaps walk backwards for a while

then lie down:
they will know where to find me

God's angle

Looking suspiciously at God,
she wonders:
What is his angle?

He says he loves her
but he keeps watching her
as if to catch her out

Maybe he wants
to take her in his arms
and hold her

protecting her from harm,
but she has been told to beware
of strangers

His motives are not clear:
she has to take charge,
protect herself, create her own worlds

Looking lovingly at her,
God wonders
if she will ever smile at him

Anne Boleyn's window

From where I am sitting I can see
Anne Boleyn's bedroom window:
I am sipping tea, keeping my head
while children plot delaying tactics
by the drawbridge

Beyond the castle
in the gardens
there is a lake and waterfalls,
an African queen, a quasi-Roman ruin and a Japanese pagoda:
we have moved on

Inside, the old portraits are flat and lifeless,
all passion scraped away
We can paint life now:
Tudor passions drifted downstream
and no longer matter, at least on the surface

Anne dreamed of love:
she dreamed of God too –
she drove a hard bargain

I see the dreams through her bedroom window
sparkling in the sun
as the schoolchildren pour out of the souvenir shop
with their toy swords

Instruments of torture
remain in the castle corridors,
and schools have been cleared of ambitious girls,
career paths redirected,
away from kings
and into television

Any girl who prayed eight times a day today
would be considered extreme, at risk,
radicalised,
cast off by Ofsted,
head down,
requiring improvement

Seagull

The seagull soars above the trees
lit from below by morning sun
bright white on blue as I look up:
for me the day has just begun –

sharp shadows creep along the street
and I am tired from the night:
the glass beneath my finger holds,
preventing me from taking flight

But something in me leaps to see
the white and blue entangled there
beyond my ordinary path:
untouchable, transcendent air

And while I reach for tea and toast
a king is heading for the coast

Song for a moment

Leonard Cohen takes years
to write a song
Bob Dylan
takes minutes

On the hills above Loch Muick
searching for gold
the path is steep but gentle

We take it easy until
a midnight cloud like a slug
slides over the summit

then I follow you down, baby
with wings to the distant village
so far away
so many years

as the hard rain catches us
you race ahead
and I pause to look back
at the angry loch

silver and salt
shadows and gold
diamonds and rust
you just out of sight

and suddenly the song is there
in an instant
no warning

I trip on an ancient rock
and forget to write it down

New year

I lie in a cooling bath on New Year's Day
thinking about redemption,
unresolved

Outside the streets are empty,
reluctant to make a start:
the sky is gallows grey, and
a half-read novel slumps on the mat

Downstairs scraps of food
wait to be cast out,
but it is too early:
my head is unprepared

The future strolls past,
glances in
and ambles onwards

It is time to wash my thinning hair:
I persuade the last shampoo
into my right hand,
knowing and forgetting
last year's bottle is now empty

I shrug, and the water ripples:
I take the bottle in my weak left fingers
and throw it across the room
towards the bin:
an impossible shot

It goes in
without
touching
the sides

It is a new year:
there is nothing I cannot do

Boneland

Sometimes I step out of the wood
on to a straw-covered path:
a warm wind brushes the hill

Sometimes the woodland ways are too steep,
and the square, unbedded stones
bite into my sole

Sometimes I go on and
sometimes I go back
looking for a place so thin that
even I cannot mistake it

Always there is
the witching wood, and
I am knot-lost,
confronted by an angel who knows
the time and the place
and will uncover me

Feeling not despair but desire,
I recognise boneland,
the place of transition
where the turbulence of time
ebbs like a lackadaisical tide

and leaves me stretched
helplessly on the bare beach
holding on to godliness
but surrounded by demons

and the fishes of galilee:
trodden on,
transformed

The rise and fall

Today, when we arrived,
the wind turned to the north
and the tide was high:
a harrier patrolled the marsh,
and you were searching
for that forgotten outer island
full of skulls and dreams and stepping stones

It was never here,
despite the emptiness that drew you: lost saints were not reported
in this estuary
though paths were flooded often enough,
and mistakes were made too

But heaven is here, or parts of it
(if heaven can be divided),
and that is why you search:
God is nearer to you
than you are yourself

So you slow down
and watch the rise and fall:
the tide will go out
further than you can see

The wind will change, and the paths will beckon –
paths only you can touch
or paint, or witness

Playing with fish

Towards evening
the same boat idles calmly into the dock,
ties up as the breeze sharpens
like the knife the net man carries to the gutting table,
surrounded by a rabble of would-be kibitzers,
mainly pelican: but a white egret and grey heron bristle
and stand firm, hogging the inner space

The knife slashes skilfully
and flesh is thrown: the right moves are made,
pieces are taken, wings slice the air:
a beak or two is satisfied

You're popular, I tell the net man
If I have fish, he replies

I have no fish, but one beak lingers on the boardwalk
wondering if there is more to me
than meets the eye,
asking itself if I am a player
or just some dead thing, uninvolved

Goats in the machine

There are goats in the machine.
I feed in fine ideas –
shining ideas,
bright software, edges cut;
you feed in transforming lines
like an angel whispering
in the world's ear

Together we could remake reality
in ice and fire

We feed in crystal-clear designs,
but there are goats in the machine:
we are chewed up and crumpled

Jammed, the machine stops

We sleep

Age of steam

Sir Nigel Gresley breathes out heavily:
his hair is white and grey
and floats around him, like memories

He pushes forward slowly,
failing to get a grip at first
as if he treads on ice

but it is summer in North Yorkshire,
and the sheep wander
aimlessly through the shops

In his prime he moved quickly,
set records like his brother

Now he dresses up, looks good,
is widely admired
(he can still pull)
but he is not required to show
all he can do

Many feel his power
first-class, first-hand:
many more watch from vantage points
outside the station
on higher ground

And I breathe out slowly
beneath thinning hair:
I remember when I moved fast
and could pull

I am not widely admired:
I do not show all I can do

I often fail to get a grip

but I can still reach
higher ground

Proof of heaven

As in a soup, spoon-hot,
I float with noodles –
the yellow tubes hold me up
and I defy gravity,
my organs mystified at the lack of pressure
from above or below

All is calm: I drift,
waiting for God to speak

Like Julian, I look for showings
of what is real – the deal
that defies description

I feel love push me
in different directions, and
my firm convictions sink:
they are too heavy

All right, I am clinging on,
but the bright white flowers
and the sun behind
make me forget all that

Grace is pouring in and out:
its currents propel me gently
from side to side

Sometimes I kick, but
I do not escape

For a while, this
is proof of heaven:
paper bark falls from birch trees
and lies on the grass, unread

Bluebell

A bluebell has flowered on my parents' grave
cradled by a caressing sun
and guarded by squirrels

Now I know that you are still alive
I can rest easy:
even the naked torsos and shiny beer cans
of oblivious passers-by
no longer provoke dead anger in me

And the apparent absence of God
does not deceive me

Hidden beneath these shadowy rows of tottering tombstones
is pure gold
the essence of something unseen
in ordinary air

righteousness dancing
in the warmth of a friendly universe,
vital signs,
raw and unmistakeable

ready to break out
and expose the facade,
destroy the conspiracy,
make everything clear

haiku

shots in the darkness
shatter dreams: splinters of light
picked up everywhere

  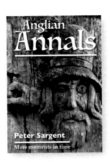 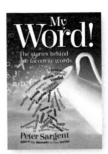

PAUL DICKSON BOOKS
Books by Norfolk writers published in Norwich

Paul Dickson has lived and worked in Norfolk for the past 33 years, initially for the National Trust, then as an independent PR practitioner and latterly as an independent publisher and tour guide.

A meeting with Illuminée Nganemariya in 2006 saw Paul assisting with Miracle in Kigali, Illuminée's story of survival during the Genocide against the Tutsis in Rwanda and subsequent life in Norwich.

After a spell as a director of Norfolk's Tagman Press, Paul decided to branch out on his own in 2016. Since then he has embarked on collaborations with Norfolk writers, Tony Ashman, Janet Collingsworth, Sandra Derry, Nicholas Groves, Steven Foyster, Neil Haverson, Tim Lenton and Peter Sargent.

  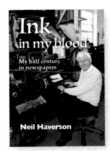 

www.pauldicksonbooks.co.uk